I0006332

CONTENTS

Chapter 1: Understanding PC Components   4

Chapter 2: Setting a Budget and Defining Your Needs   8

Chapter 3: Tools and Workspace Setup   11

Chapter 4: Choosing the Right Components   15

Chapter 5: Assembling the PC   19

Chapter 6: Installing the Operating System   27

Chapter 7: Essential Software and Drivers   31

Chapter 8: PC Maintenance and Troubleshooting   37

Chapter 9: PC Gaming and Performance Optimization   42

Chapter 10: Future-Proofing and Conclusion   48

Chapter 11: Beyond the Basics – Advanced PC Building Techniques   52

Chapter 12: The Sustainable PC Builder   57

Appendix A: PC Component Compatibility Guide   62

Appendix B: Troubleshooting Guide   64

Appendix C: Resources and Further Reading   66

Conclusion: Embark on Your PC Building Journey   68

About the Author   71

Introduction: Your Path to PC Building Mastery

Welcome to the world of PC building, where you get to be the mastermind behind your very own high-performance, customized computer. If you've ever marveled at the sleek machines powering your favorite games, handling complex tasks, or simply wanted a computer that's tailor-made for your needs, you're in for an exciting journey.

Building your own PC might seem like a daunting task, reserved for tech gurus and computer wizards. But fear not! Before you embark on this adventure, we recommend that you read through this entire book. It will be your ticket to demystifying the process and unlocking the secrets of the modern PC. Whether you're a complete beginner or a tech enthusiast looking to take your skills to the next level, we've got you covered.

Why build your own PC? Well, for starters, it's an immensely satisfying experience. Imagine piecing together cutting-edge components, turning them on, and watching your creation come to life. It's like building your own superhero suit, tailored to your specific needs and desires.

But that's not all. Building your own PC allows you to save money, as you're not paying for the markup that pre-built systems often come with. You also gain the power to choose every single component, ensuring that your PC aligns perfectly with your goals, whether that's conquering the gaming world, tackling intensive graphic design projects, or simply enjoying a smooth and fast computing experience.

In this book, we'll take you by the hand and guide you through every step of the PC building journey. We'll explain the intricacies of each component, show you how to select the best parts for your budget, and walk you through the assembly process with easy-to-follow instructions. By the end of this adventure, you'll not only have a fully functional PC but also a newfound sense of confidence and accomplishment.

So, are you ready to embark on this exciting journey and unlock the world of PC building? We encourage you to read through the entire book first to familiarize yourself with the process. Then, when you're ready, grab your toolkit, put on your builder's cap, and let's dive in. Building your own PC is not just about crafting a computer; it's about crafting your future. Let's get started!"

CHAPTER 1: UNDERSTANDING PC COMPONENTS

In the world of PC building, knowledge is your most potent tool. Before we dive into the nitty-gritty of assembling a computer, it's essential to understand the fundamental building blocks that make up a PC. Think of them as the puzzle pieces that, when put together correctly, create the magic of modern computing.

1.1 The Heart of the Machine: Central Processing Unit (CPU)

At the core of every computer is the Central Processing Unit, or CPU. It's the brain of your PC, responsible for executing instructions and performing calculations. CPUs come in various models and speeds, and selecting the right one depends on your intended use.

- **Clock Speed:** Measured in gigahertz (GHz), the clock speed determines how many instructions a CPU can execute per second. Faster is generally better for tasks like gaming and video editing.

- **Cores and Threads:** CPUs can have multiple cores and threads. Cores allow for parallel processing, and threads can further enhance multitasking capabilities. For gaming and most general tasks, a quad-core processor should suffice, but more cores can be beneficial for demanding applications.

1.2 Visual Excellence: Graphics Processing Unit (GPU)

If you plan on gaming or working with graphics-intensive applications, you'll need a dedicated Graphics Processing Unit, or GPU. The GPU handles rendering images and videos, making it crucial for a smooth visual experience.

- **Integrated vs. Discrete:** Some CPUs come with integrated graphics, suitable for everyday tasks but not for gaming or professional graphics work. For the latter, a separate, more powerful discrete GPU is necessary.

- **VRAM:** Video RAM (VRAM) stores textures and other data needed for rendering. A GPU with more VRAM can handle higher-resolution textures and complex scenes.

1.3 Memory Matters: Random Access Memory (RAM)

RAM is your computer's short-term memory. It stores data that the CPU is actively using, allowing for quick access. The amount of RAM you need depends on your usage, but 8GB is generally a good starting point for most users.

- **DDR4 vs. DDR5**: Pay attention to the RAM generation (DDR4 or DDR5) and its speed (measured in MHz) for optimal performance. Faster RAM can enhance overall system responsiveness.

1.4 Data Storage Solutions

Storage options have evolved significantly, offering a variety of choices to suit different needs:

- **Solid State Drives (SSD):** Lightning-fast storage that enhances boot times and application loading. Consider using an SSD as your primary drive.

- **Hard Disk Drives (HDD):** Offer large storage capacity at a lower cost but are slower compared to SSDs. Useful for storing media and files that don't require high-speed access.

1.5 Motherboard: The Nervous System

The motherboard is the backbone of your PC, connecting all components and allowing them to communicate. When choosing a motherboard, consider factors like CPU socket compatibility, RAM slots, available ports for future expansion, and its chipset, which affects features like USB support and overclocking capabilities.

1.6 Powering Your PC: The

Power Supply Unit (PSU)

Every PC needs a reliable source of power, and that's where the Power Supply Unit (PSU) comes in. The PSU converts electricity from your wall outlet into a form that your PC can use. Here are some key considerations:

- **Wattage:** The wattage rating of a PSU determines how much power it can deliver to your components. To determine your PSU's wattage requirements, add up the power requirements of your CPU, GPU, and other components. It's wise to go slightly above this total to allow for future upgrades.

- **Efficiency Rating:** PSUs come with efficiency ratings like 80 PLUS Bronze, Silver, Gold, Platinum, or Titanium. Higher ratings indicate better efficiency and lower energy waste.

- **Modularity:** Modular PSUs allow you to attach only the cables you need, reducing clutter and improving airflow inside your case.

Understanding these core components, including the Power Supply Unit, is the first step in your PC building journey. As you explore the world of PC hardware, keep in mind that each component plays a unique role in shaping your computer's performance and capabilities. In the following chapters, we'll dive deeper into each of these components, helping you make informed decisions to create the PC of your dreams. Stay curious and excited because the adventure has just begun!

CHAPTER 2:
SETTING A BUDGET AND DEFINING YOUR NEEDS

In the exhilarating journey of building your own PC, one of the first and most crucial steps is to determine your budget and precisely define your needs. Why? Because these factors will serve as your guiding lights throughout the entire process, ensuring that you end up with a computer that's not only tailored to your desires but also doesn't break the bank.

2.1 The Importance of
Setting a Budget

Before you dive headfirst into the world of PC component shopping, it's essential to establish a clear budget. Your budget serves as the financial boundary within which you'll be working. Here's why it matters:

- **Cost Control**: A budget helps you keep your spending in check. Without it, you might be tempted to splurge on unnecessary features or components.

- **Avoiding Overspending:** Building a PC can quickly become an expensive endeavor if you're not mindful. Having a budget prevents you from overspending and experiencing buyer's remorse.

2.2 Defining Your PC's Purpose

Once you've set your budget, the next step is to define precisely what you want your PC to do. The purpose of your PC will heavily influence the components you select. Here are some common purposes for building a PC:

- **Gaming:** If your primary goal is gaming, you'll want to prioritize a powerful GPU, sufficient RAM, and a fast CPU. Consider the types of games you play and the desired graphics settings.

- **Content Creation:** For tasks like video editing, 3D rendering, or graphic design,
  focus on a robust CPU, ample RAM, and storage with high read/write speeds.

- **Office/Productivity:** If you need a PC for everyday tasks, such as web browsing, word processing, and email, you can opt for more budget-friendly components.

- **Home Theater PC (HTPC):** Building a PC for your home theater system may require a compact case and components with quiet operation.

2.3 Future-Proofing Considerations

When defining your PC's purpose, also consider its longevity. Do you want a PC that will remain relevant for several years, or are you comfortable with the idea of upgrading sooner? Future-proofing considerations include:

- **Component Compatibility:** Ensure that your motherboard and case can accommodate potential future upgrades, like additional RAM, storage drives, or a more powerful GPU.

- **Overclocking Capability:** If you're interested in overclocking, invest in components that support it, such as a "K" series Intel CPU or an unlocked AMD processor.

- **Expandability:** Opt for a motherboard with extra PCIe slots, USB ports, and RAM slots if you anticipate adding more components down the line.

- **Power Supply Headroom:** Select a PSU with a wattage slightly higher than your current needs to accommodate future upgrades without having to replace it.

By setting a budget and defining your PC's purpose, you're establishing a solid foundation for your PC building project. These early decisions will guide your component choices and ensure that you create a computer that not only meets your immediate needs but also aligns with your long-term goals.

In the following chapters, we'll dive deeper into each component category, helping you make informed decisions based on your budget and purpose. Your journey to building the perfect PC is well underway, so stay tuned for more insights and guidance!

CHAPTER 3: TOOLS AND WORKSPACE SETUP

Before you can start assembling your dream PC, you'll need to prepare your workspace and gather the necessary tools. Building a PC is like constructing a work of art; it requires precision, organization, and the right environment. In this chapter, we'll cover the tools and workspace setup required for a smooth and successful PC build.

3.1 Essential Tools for PC Building

Building a PC doesn't require a vast array of tools, but having the right ones is crucial for a stress-free experience. Here are the essential tools you'll need:

- **Screwdriver:** A Phillips-head screwdriver is the most commonly used tool. It's used to secure components like the motherboard, power supply, and storage drives to your case.

- **Anti-static Wrist Strap:** This strap helps discharge any static electricity from your body, preventing potential damage to sensitive components like your CPU or RAM. It's an important tool, especially in dry environments.

- **Cable Ties or Velcro Straps:** These are used for cable management, keeping your internal components tidy and improving airflow for better cooling.

- **Needle-Nose Pliers:** Handy for reaching tight spaces or bending stubborn metal tabs on your case or components.

- **Flashlight:** Good lighting is essential, and a flashlight can help you see into the nooks and crannies of your PC case.

- **Small Parts Organizer:** Keep screws, standoffs, and other small components organized and easily accessible.

3.2 Preparing Your Workspace

A clean and organized workspace is essential for an efficient and trouble-free PC build. Here's how to set up your workspace:

- **Clear a Large Work Surface:** Ensure you have enough space to lay out your components and tools. A large, clean table or desk is ideal.

- **Static-Free Zone:** Build on a non-static surface like a wooden table or an anti-static mat. Avoid working on carpets, as they can generate static electricity.

- **Good Lighting:** Adequate lighting is crucial for seeing fine details. Position your workspace near a window or use bright, adjustable LED lights.

- **Clean Environment:** Keep your workspace free of dust and debris. Dust can settle on your components, potentially causing overheating and performance issues.

3.3 Safety Precautions

Safety is a top priority when working with electronic components. Follow these precautions to protect yourself and your components:

- **Turn Off the Power:** Before handling any components, unplug your PC and turn off the power supply switch (if applicable). This prevents electrical accidents.

- **Wear ESD Protection:** Always wear an anti-static wrist strap to prevent electrostatic discharge, which can damage sensitive components.

- **Work Slowly and Carefully:** Rushing can lead to mistakes. Take your time, read instructions, and double-check connections.

- **Avoid Magnetic Fields:** Keep magnetic devices (like strong magnets and magnetic screwdrivers) away from sensitive components like hard drives and SSDs, as they can erase data.

- **Handle Components Carefully:** Be gentle when inserting or removing components. Avoid applying excessive force, which can damage connectors or sockets.

By preparing your workspace, gathering essential tools, and following safety precautions, you'll create the ideal environment for building your PC. In the next chapters, we'll dive deeper into selecting and assembling specific components, turning your vision of the perfect PC into a reality. Stay organized, stay safe, and enjoy the journey of building your own computer!

CHAPTER 4:
CHOOSING THE RIGHT COMPONENTS

Building a PC is like assembling a puzzle, and the quality of your finished product depends on the individual pieces you select. In this chapter, we'll delve into the critical components that form the heart and soul of your computer. By the end of this chapter, you'll have a clear understanding of how to choose the right components for your needs and budget.

4.1 The CPU (Central Processing Unit)

The CPU is the brain of your computer, responsible for executing instructions and performing calculations. Here's what to consider when choosing one:

- **Performance vs. Budget:** CPUs come in various models and price ranges. Decide how much processing power you need based on your usage (gaming, content creation, general tasks) and budget.

- **Clock Speed and Cores:** Higher clock speeds are better for tasks that rely on single-threaded performance, like gaming. More cores are beneficial for multitasking and CPU-intensive applications.

- **Brand and Compatibility:** Check the CPU socket compatibility with your selected motherboard, and decide between Intel and AMD based on your needs and preferences.

4.2 The GPU (Graphics Processing Unit)

The GPU handles rendering graphics, making it crucial for gaming and graphics-intensive tasks. Consider these factors when choosing a GPU:

- **Performance vs. Resolution:** Choose a GPU that can handle your desired gaming resolution and graphics settings. Higher-end GPUs are necessary for 4K gaming, while mid-range options are suitable for 1080p.

- **VRAM:** Video RAM (VRAM) stores textures and data for rendering. More VRAM is essential for high-resolution gaming and content creation tasks.

- **Brand and Budget:** NVIDIA and AMD offer GPUs at various price points. Select one that aligns with your budget and performance requirements.

4.3 Memory (RAM)

RAM is your computer's short-term memory, crucial for multitasking and running applications smoothly. Consider these factors when choosing RAM:

- **Capacity:** 8GB is a minimum for most users, but consider 16GB or more for gaming and content creation.

- **Speed:** Faster RAM (measured in MHz) can improve overall system performance, especially with integrated graphics or AMD Ryzen CPUs.

- **Compatibility:** Ensure your RAM is compatible with your motherboard's specifications, including DDR4 or DDR5 compatibility.

4.4 Storage Drives

Selecting the right storage drives is essential for fast system performance and data storage. Here are your options:

- **Solid State Drives (SSD):** SSDs offer blazing-fast speeds and are ideal for your operating system and frequently used applications. Consider an NVMe SSD for even faster performance.

- **Hard Disk Drives (HDD):** HDDs provide large storage capacities at a lower cost, suitable for storing files and media.

- **Hybrid Drives:** Some drives combine SSD and HDD technologies, offering a compromise between speed and storage capacity.

- **M.2 SSD:** M.2 SSDs are a type of SSD that plugs directly into your motherboard, reducing cable clutter. They come in various lengths and offer exceptional speed, making them an excellent choice for your operating system and applications.

4.5 Motherboard

The motherboard connects all your components and plays a crucial role in your PC's functionality. Consider these factors when choosing a motherboard:

- **CPU Socket Compatibility:** Ensure the motherboard supports your chosen CPU's socket type (e.g., LGA 1200, AM4).

- **Form Factor:** Select a motherboard size (ATX, Micro ATX, Mini ITX) that fits your case and provides the desired expansion options.

- **Features:** Motherboards vary in features like Wi-Fi support, USB ports, M.2 slots, and overclocking capabilities.

4.6 Power Supply Unit (PSU)

Your PSU converts electricity into power your PC can use. When selecting a PSU:

- **Wattage:** Calculate the power requirements of your components and choose a PSU with a wattage slightly higher than needed to allow for future upgrades.

- **Efficiency:** Higher efficiency ratings (e.g., 80 PLUS Bronze, Gold, Platinum) are more energy-efficient and generate less heat.

- **Modularity:** Modular PSUs allow you to connect only the cables you need, reducing clutter and improving airflow.

Understanding these key components and their considerations is crucial for creating a PC that matches your performance needs, budget, and long-term goals. In the next chapters, we'll explore the assembly process, step-by-step, ensuring that you bring all these components together to build a powerful and functional PC.

CHAPTER 5:
ASSEMBLING THE PC

Now that you've carefully selected the components for your dream PC, it's time to roll up your sleeves and start putting it all together. Building a PC is like assembling a high-tech jigsaw puzzle, and in this chapter, we'll guide you step by step through the assembly process. By the end of this chapter, you'll have a fully functional PC ready to power up.

5.1 Pre-Assembly Preparations

Before you start assembling your PC, make sure you have everything you need ready:

- **Components:** Ensure all your chosen components are at hand. Double-check for any missing items.

- **Tools:** Have your essential tools, including a screwdriver, anti-static wrist strap, cable ties, and pliers, within reach.

- **Workspace:** Your clean and well-lit workspace should be ready with adequate room to lay out your components.

- **Safety First:** Remember to wear your anti-static wrist strap and follow safety precautions from Chapter 3.

5.2 Step-by-Step Assembly Process

Let's break down the assembly process into manageable steps:

Step 1: Prepare the Case

1. Lay your PC case flat on your workspace with the side panel removed.
2. Install the I/O shield (included with your motherboard) into the rear of the case. Ensure it's properly aligned with the motherboard ports.

Step 2: Mount the Power Supply Unit (PSU)

1. Place the PSU into the PSU compartment of the case with the fan facing down (for optimal cooling).
2. Secure the PSU with screws through the back of the case.

Step 3: Install the Motherboard

1. Gently place your motherboard into the case, aligning the I/O ports with the I/O shield.
2. Secure the motherboard to the case using screws provided with the case (typically, 6-9 screws).

Step 4: Install the CPU and CPU Cooler

1. Open the CPU socket on the motherboard and gently place the CPU into it, aligning the notches or markings.
2. Close the socket lever to secure the CPU.
3. Apply thermal paste to the CPU if your CPU cooler doesn't have pre-applied paste.
4. Attach the CPU cooler to the CPU socket using the provided brackets or mounts and secure it with screws.

Step 5: Install RAM (Memory)

1. Open the RAM slots on the motherboard.
2. Align the notch on your RAM sticks with the slot on the motherboard and gently press down until the clips on each side click into place.

Step 6: Install Storage Drives

1. For SSDs or HDDs, locate the drive bays in your case, and secure the drives using screws or drive trays provided with your case.

2. For M.2 SSDs, find the M.2 slots on your motherboard and insert the M.2 SSD at a 30-degree angle. Secure it with a screw provided on the motherboard.

Step 7: Connect Power Cables

1. Connect the main 24-pin ATX power cable from the PSU to the motherboard.
2. Connect the 4/8-pin CPU power cable from the PSU to the motherboard.
3. Connect power cables from the PSU to your storage drives.

Step 8: Connect Data Cables

1. Connect SATA data cables from the motherboard to your storage drives (SSDs/HDDs).
2. Connect front panel connectors (power switch, reset switch, LEDs, USB ports, audio) to the motherboard using your motherboard's manual as a guide.

Pay Attention to Polarity: Power LED, HDD LED, and speaker connectors often have polarity, meaning they have a positive (+) and negative (-) wire. Pay close attention to the positive and negative markings on both the connectors and the motherboard's front panel header.

Step 9: Cable Management

Use cable ties or Velcro straps to bundle and secure cables, keeping them organized and out of the way for proper airflow.

Step 10: Install Graphics Card (GPU)

If you have a dedicated GPU, insert it into a PCIe slot on the motherboard and secure it with the PCIe bracket latch. Connect the GPU power cables from the PSU.

Step 11: Final Checks

Double-check all connections, ensuring that everything is properly seated and connected.

Step 12: Close the Case

Put the side panel back on the case and secure it with screws.

5.3 Tips for installing new fans
and optimizing airflow

Proper airflow management is essential for maintaining optimal temperatures and maximizing the performance of your custom-built PC. Whether you're upgrading your existing cooling setup or adding new fans, here are some tips to help you get the most out of your airflow:

1. Plan Your Airflow: Before installing new fans, consider the overall airflow direction in your case. Typically, air should flow from the front to the back and top to bottom. This setup ensures that cool air enters at the front and is exhausted at the rear and top, carrying away heat.

2. Balance Intake and Exhaust: Achieve a balance between intake and exhaust fans to maintain positive air pressure inside the case. Positive pressure reduces the buildup of dust and helps cool components more effectively. A typical setup includes more intake fans than exhaust fans.

3. Position Your Fans Strategically: Place intake fans at the front or side of the case to draw in cool air, and exhaust fans at the rear and top to expel hot air. Consider using fan filters on intake fans to prevent dust buildup.

4. Size Matters: Choose fans of the appropriate size for your case's fan mounts. Common sizes include 120mm and 140mm. Larger fans can move more air with less noise, but check your case's compatibility.

5. Consider Static Pressure: If you have components with dense fin arrays (e.g., radiators or heatsinks), consider fans designed for high static pressure. These fans can push air through tight spaces more effectively.

6. Cable Management: Neatly route fan cables to avoid obstructing airflow. Use cable ties or Velcro straps to secure cables out of the way.

7. Monitor Temperatures: Keep an eye on component temperatures using monitoring software. This helps you identify cooling inefficiencies and make necessary adjustments.

8. GPU Orientation: If your GPU has multiple fans, consider orienting it so that it expels hot air out of the case rather than recirculating it inside.

9. Experiment with Fan Speeds: Most motherboards allow you to adjust fan speeds through the BIOS/UEFI settings or dedicated software. Experiment with fan curves to find the right balance between cooling and noise levels.

10. Dust Management: Regularly clean dust filters and internal components to maintain airflow efficiency. Dust can accumulate over time and lead to higher temperatures.

11. Upgrade Case Fans: If your case came with stock fans, consider upgrading to higher-quality fans for better airflow and quieter operation. Look for fans with low noise levels and high airflow ratings.

12. Silicon Gel or Rubber Mounts: Use rubber or silicone mounts for fans to reduce vibration and noise. These mounts can help isolate fans from the case and minimize vibrations.

13. Positive Airflow Through Components: Ensure that cool air flows over critical components like the CPU and GPU. Position fans to direct air where it's needed most.

By following these tips, you can achieve efficient airflow management in your PC, leading to improved cooling performance and a quieter computing experience. Proper airflow not only prolongs the life of your components but also enhances overall system stability and reliability.

5.4 First Boot and Testing

With your PC assembled, it's time for the moment of truth:

1. Plug in your monitor, keyboard, and mouse.

2 Connect the power cable to your PSU and the wall outlet.

3. Press the power button to boot up your PC.

4. If all goes well, you should see your motherboard's BIOS/UEFI screen. Follow the on-screen instructions to set up your BIOS settings and install the operating system.

5. If there are any issues, refer to Chapter 8 on troubleshooting common PC problems.

Congratulations! You've successfully assembled your own PC. In the next chapters, we'll cover installing the operating system, configuring your PC, and maintaining it for optimal performance. Your custom-built PC is now ready to unleash its power and fulfill your computing dreams.

CHAPTER 6:
INSTALLING THE
OPERATING SYSTEM

With your custom-built PC up and running, it's time to breathe life into it by installing an operating system (OS). The OS is the software that manages hardware resources, runs applications, and provides you with a user-friendly interface. In this chapter, we'll walk you through the process of installing an OS on your new PC.

6.1 Choosing an Operating System

Before diving into the installation process, you need to decide which operating system you want to use. Here are some popular options:

- **Windows 10 or 11:** Microsoft's Windows OS is widely used and suitable for gaming, productivity, and general computing. Be sure to have a valid product key for activation.

- **Linux:** Linux distributions like Ubuntu, Fedora, or Debian are free and open-source options that offer robust security and customization. They're great for developers and those looking for a more lightweight OS.

6.2 Preparing Installation Media

To install an OS, you'll need installation media, typically in the form of a bootable USB drive or DVD. Here's how to create installation media:

Creating Bootable Media:

1. **Windows:**
- Download the Windows Media Creation Tool from the official Microsoft website.
- Follow the tool's instructions to create a bootable USB drive with the Windows OS of your choice.

2. **Linux:**
- Download the ISO image of your preferred Linux distribution from its official website.
- Create a bootable USB drive using a tool like Rufus (for Windows) or Etcher (for macOS and Linux).

Why Bootable Media?

Creating bootable media allows you to install the OS on your PC from scratch. It's particularly useful for new builds, as it ensures a clean installation without any residual data from a previous OS.

6.3 Installing the Operating System

Now that you have your installation media ready, it's time to install the OS:

1. Boot from Installation Media:

- Insert the bootable USB drive or DVD into your PC.
- Restart your PC, and during the boot process, access the BIOS/UEFI settings (usually by pressing a key like F2 or Delete).
- In the BIOS/UEFI settings, change the boot order to prioritize the installation media (USB drive or DVD drive) as the first boot device.
- Save the changes and exit the BIOS/UEFI settings.

2. OS Installation:

- Your PC should now boot from the installation media. Follow the on-screen instructions to start the OS installation process.
- Choose your language, time zone, and keyboard layout when prompted.

Partitioning and Formatting:

Why Partitioning Might Be a Good Idea:

Partitioning involves dividing your storage drive into separate sections, or partitions, each acting as a virtual drive. Here's why partitioning might be a good idea:

- **Organization:** Partitioning allows you to organize your data more effectively. For example, you can have one partition for the OS and applications, another for personal files, and possibly more for backup or different OS installations.

- **Backup and Recovery:** By separating your OS and data into different partitions, you can back up critical data more easily without affecting the OS itself. In case of OS issues, you can reinstall the OS on its partition without losing your data.

- **Performance:** Partitioning can help improve performance by isolating certain types of data. For example, keeping multimedia files on a separate partition can prevent fragmentation and improve file access speed.

1. **Product Key and Activation:**
- If installing Windows, enter your valid product key when prompted.

2. **Completing the Installation:**
- Once the installation process is complete, your PC will prompt you to remove the installation media and restart.

3. **Post-Installation Setup:**
- After the restart, follow the on-screen setup prompts to configure your user account, network settings, and other preferences.

6.4 Driver Installation

After installing the OS, it's essential to install drivers to ensure that all your hardware components work correctly. Check the manufacturer's website for your motherboard and GPU for the latest drivers. For Windows, the OS may automatically detect and install some drivers, but it's a good practice to install the latest ones from the manufacturer's website for optimal performance.

Congratulations! You've successfully installed the operating system on your custom-built PC. In the next chapters, we'll cover essential software, configuration, and maintenance tasks to ensure your PC runs smoothly and efficiently.

CHAPTER 7:
ESSENTIAL SOFTWARE AND DRIVERS

Now that you have your operating system up and running on your custom-built PC, it's time to ensure that it's equipped with the necessary software and drivers. In this chapter, we'll guide you through the installation of essential software, including drivers, to optimize your PC's performance and functionality.

7.1 Installing Essential Software

To make the most of your PC, you'll need a set of essential software applications. Here are some key software categories to consider:

1. Web Browser:

- Install a web browser like Google Chrome, Mozilla Firefox, or Microsoft Edge to access the internet and browse websites.

2. Office Suite:

- For productivity tasks, consider installing an office suite like Microsoft Office, LibreOffice, or Google Workspace for document editing, spreadsheets, and presentations.

3. Antivirus Software:

- Protect your PC from malware and viruses with reliable antivirus software like Bitdefender, McAfee, or Windows Defender (pre-installed on Windows).

4. Media Players:

- Install media players such as VLC Media Player or Windows Media Player for audio and video playback.

5. PDF Reader:

- A PDF reader like Adobe Acrobat Reader is essential for viewing and working with PDF documents.

6. Compression and Archiving Tools:

- Applications like 7-Zip or WinRAR allow you to compress and extract files and folders.

7. Image Editing Software:

- If you work with images, consider applications like Adobe Photoshop, GIMP, or Paint.NET.

8. Backup and Recovery Tools:

- Set up backup software like Acronis True Image, Macrium Reflect, or Windows Backup to safeguard your data.

9. Messaging and Communication:

- Install communication apps like Skype, Slack, or Discord for staying in touch with friends and colleagues.

10. Additional Software: -

- Depending on your needs, you may want to install specialized software for tasks like video editing, programming, or gaming.

7.2 Driver Installation

Drivers are essential pieces of software that allow your hardware components to communicate effectively with the operating system. Here's how to install drivers for your PC:

1. Graphics Drivers:

- Visit the website of your GPU manufacturer (NVIDIA or AMD) to download and install the latest graphics drivers. Up-to-date graphics drivers are crucial for gaming and graphical performance.

2. Motherboard Drivers:

- Head to the motherboard manufacturer's website to download and install the latest drivers for your motherboard. This includes drivers for audio, Ethernet, and other onboard components.

3. Peripheral Drivers:

- If you have additional peripherals like printers, scanners, or webcams, visit the manufacturers' websites to download and install the necessary drivers.

4. Windows Update:

- Windows Update often includes driver updates. Check for updates in the Windows settings to ensure your OS has the latest drivers.

7.3 Software Updates

Keeping your software up to date is essential for security and performance. Most software applications, including your operating system, have built-in update mechanisms. Here's how to ensure your software is current:

- **Windows Updates:** In Windows, go to Settings > Update & Security > Windows Update to check for and install updates.

- **Third-Party Software Updates:** Many applications have an "Check for Updates" option in their menus. Alternatively, you can use software like Patch My PC or Chocolatey to automate the updating of third-party applications.

7.4 Customizing Your Desktop

With your software and drivers in place, it's time to make your PC truly your own. Customize your desktop by:

- **Choosing a Wallpaper:** Set your favorite wallpaper or select a theme that reflects your style.
- **Organizing Icons**: Arrange desktop icons for quick access to frequently used applications and files.
- **Configuring Start Menu/Taskbar**: Customize the Start Menu and Taskbar to include shortcuts to your preferred apps.
- **Personalizing Settings:** Adjust system settings, such as display preferences, sound, and notifications.

7.5 Security Measures

Don't forget to prioritize your PC's security:

- Activate Your Antivirus: Ensure your antivirus software is active and receiving updates.
- Firewall Settings: Configure your firewall to protect against unauthorized access.
- Regular Backups: Set up automated backups to safeguard your important files.
- Strong Passwords: Use strong, unique passwords for your user account and online services.

By installing essential software, updating drivers, customizing your desktop, and maintaining security measures, you'll maximize your PC's functionality and security. In the next chapters, we'll explore advanced topics such as overclocking, troubleshooting, and maintenance to ensure your PC stays in top shape.

CHAPTER 8: PC MAINTENANCE AND TROUBLESHOOTING

Congratulations on successfully building your custom PC and setting up the essential software! However, your journey as a PC builder doesn't end here. In this chapter, we'll cover the importance of regular maintenance, common PC issues, and how to troubleshoot them to keep your computer running smoothly.

8.1 Regular PC Maintenance

Routine maintenance can extend the life and performance of your PC. Here are some essential maintenance tasks to consider:

1. **Cleaning**:
   - Regularly clean dust from your PC's interior using compressed air. Dust buildup can cause overheating and reduce performance.

2. **Software Updates:**
   - Keep your operating system and software applications up to date to ensure security and performance improvements.

3. **Disk Cleanup:**
   - Use the built-in Windows Disk Cleanup tool or third-party software to remove temporary files and free up disk space.

4. **Disk Defragmentation (HDDs only):**
   - If you're using a traditional hard disk drive (HDD), consider defragmenting it periodically to optimize file storage.

5. **Backup:**
   - Regularly back up your important files to an external drive or cloud storage to safeguard against data loss.

6. **Check for Malware:**
   - Run regular scans with your antivirus software to detect and remove malware.

8.2 Troubleshooting
Common PC Issues

No PC is immune to problems. Knowing how to troubleshoot common issues can save you time and frustration. Here are some typical problems and their solutions:

1. Slow Performance:
- Close unused applications and browser tabs.
- Check for resource-hungry processes in Task Manager.
- Upgrade hardware components like RAM or storage for a speed boost.

2. Blue Screen of Death (BSOD):
- Note the error code displayed on the BSOD for troubleshooting.
- Update or reinstall faulty drivers.
- Check for hardware issues like RAM or overheating.

3. No Display on Monitor:
- Ensure all cables are securely connected.
- Test the monitor and cables on another device.
- If using a dedicated GPU, make sure it's properly seated in the PCIe slot.

4. Overheating:
- Ensure adequate airflow inside the case.
- Clean dust from fans and heat sinks.
- Apply high-quality thermal paste between the CPU and cooler.

5. Software Crashes:
- Update or reinstall the problematic software.
- Check for conflicts between software applications.
- Scan for malware that may be causing instability.

6. Internet Connection Issues:
- Restart your router and modem.

- Check for loose cables and try a wired connection if possible.
- Contact your ISP for assistance with connection problems.

7. Noisy Fans:
- Clean or replace dusty or malfunctioning fans.
- Adjust fan curves in the BIOS/UEFI settings to reduce noise.

8.3 Advanced Maintenance
and Upgrades

For advanced users looking to enhance their PC's performance, consider these options:

1. Overclocking:
- Overclocking your CPU or GPU can provide a performance boost. However, it requires careful tuning and monitoring to avoid overheating and instability.

2. Hardware Upgrades:
- As your needs change, consider upgrading hardware components such as RAM, storage, or the GPU for improved performance.

3. Backup Strategies:
- Implement robust backup strategies, including both local and offsite backups, for data protection.

4. System Optimization:
- Fine-tune your operating system settings for better performance and responsiveness.

5. Custom Cooling Solutions:
- Consider advanced cooling solutions like liquid cooling for better temperature control, especially if you're overclocking.

By performing regular maintenance and being prepared to troubleshoot common issues, you can ensure that your custom-built PC continues to provide the performance and reliability you expect. In the following chapters, we'll delve into more advanced topics, helping you make the most of your PC and explore the exciting world of PC gaming.

CHAPTER 9: PC GAMING AND PERFORMANCE OPTIMIZATION

If you're a gaming enthusiast or looking to optimize your PC's performance for specific tasks, this chapter is for you. We'll explore the world of PC gaming, performance optimization, and how to get the most out of your custom-built PC.

9.1 PC Gaming

Gaming on a custom-built PC can be an exhilarating experience. Here are some key considerations for PC gaming:

1. Graphics Settings:
- Adjust in-game graphics settings to balance visual quality and performance. Options often include resolution, texture quality, shadows, and anti-aliasing.

2. Game Library:
- Explore the wide range of games available on PC through platforms like Steam, Epic Games Store, and GOG.

3. Gaming Peripherals:
- Invest in quality gaming peripherals, such as a gaming keyboard, mouse, and headset, for a more immersive experience.

4. Game Streaming:
- If interested in game streaming, explore services like Twitch or YouTube Gaming and consider dedicated streaming hardware or software.

5. GPU Drivers:
- Keep your GPU drivers up to date to ensure optimal performance and compatibility with the latest games.

6. Modding Community:
- Many PC games have active modding communities that enhance gameplay, graphics, and content. Explore mods that interest you.

9.2 Performance Optimization

Optimizing your PC's performance can help you get the most out of your hardware. Here are some tips for performance optimization:

1. Overclocking:
- If you're comfortable with it, consider overclocking your CPU and GPU to boost performance. However, be cautious and monitor temperatures to prevent overheating.

2. SSD for Storage:
- If you're using a traditional HDD, consider upgrading to an SSD for faster load times and system responsiveness.

3. RAM Expansion:
- Adding more RAM can improve multitasking and the performance of memory-intensive applications.

4. Graphics Card Upgrade:
- For gaming and graphics-intensive tasks, upgrading your GPU can have a significant impact on performance.

5. Disk Cleanup:
- Regularly remove unnecessary files and applications to free up storage space and improve system performance.

6. Defragmentation (HDDs only):
- If you have an HDD, defragment it periodically to optimize file storage.

7. Disable Startup Programs:
- Disable unnecessary startup programs that can slow down your PC's boot time.

8. Background Applications:
- Close or disable background applications and processes that consume system resources.

9. Power Plan Settings:

- Adjust your power plan settings to prioritize performance over power savings when needed.

10. Monitor Refresh Rate: - If you have a high-refresh-rate monitor, make sure your games are set to run at the monitor's maximum refresh rate for smoother gameplay.

9.3 PC Hardware Upgrades

Upgrading specific hardware components can have a substantial impact on your PC's performance:

1. GPU Upgrade:
- Upgrading to a more powerful GPU can enhance gaming performance and support higher resolutions and graphics settings.

2. SSD Addition:
- Adding an additional SSD for games and applications can improve load times and overall system responsiveness.

3. RAM Expansion:
- Increasing your RAM capacity is beneficial for multitasking and running memory-intensive applications.

4. CPU Upgrade:
- Consider upgrading your CPU if you need more processing power for tasks like video editing or 3D rendering.

5. Cooling Solutions:
- Invest in advanced cooling solutions like liquid cooling for overclocking and temperature control.

9.4 Maintenance for Gamers

For gamers, maintaining your PC is essential for uninterrupted gameplay:

1. Regular Cleaning:
- Dust can accumulate quickly in gaming PCs. Regularly clean fans and components to prevent overheating.

2. Game Updates:
- Keep your games up to date to benefit from bug fixes, performance improvements, and new content.

3. Driver Updates:
- Stay current with GPU drivers for the latest game optimizations and compatibility.

4. Temperature Monitoring:
- Use software tools to monitor CPU and GPU temperatures during gaming sessions.

5. Backup Saves:
- Regularly back up your game saves to prevent data loss in case of hardware failure.

By following these gaming and performance optimization tips and staying up to date with hardware upgrades, you'll ensure that your custom-built PC delivers top-notch performance and an outstanding gaming experience. Enjoy your gaming adventures!

CHAPTER 10: FUTURE-PROOFING AND CONCLUSION

In this final chapter, we'll explore the concept of future-proofing your custom-built PC and wrap up your journey as a PC builder.

10.1 Future-Proofing Your PC

Technology is constantly evolving, and while you can't future-proof a PC indefinitely, you can take steps to extend its longevity and adaptability
:

1. Upgrade Path:
- When selecting components, consider those that allow for future upgrades. Look for motherboards with extra PCIe slots, RAM slots, and CPU socket compatibility.

2. High-Quality Components:
- Invest in quality components that are less likely to become obsolete quickly.

3. Expandable Storage:
- Opt for a larger case that can accommodate additional storage drives and expansion cards.

4. Overclocking:
- If you're comfortable with overclocking, it can provide a performance boost and extend your PC's usable life.

5. Monitor Compatibility:
- When upgrading your GPU, ensure it supports the latest monitor technologies, such as high refresh rates, resolutions, and adaptive sync.

6. Modular PSU:
- Consider a modular power supply unit (PSU) that allows you to add or remove cables as needed for future upgrades.

7. Regular Maintenance:
- Continue to perform regular maintenance to keep your PC running smoothly and extend its life.

10.2 Conclusion: Your Custom-Built PC Journey

Building your own PC is an empowering and rewarding experience. You've embarked on a journey to create a personalized computing powerhouse tailored to your needs and preferences. Along the way, you've learned about selecting components, assembly, installing an operating system, maintaining and troubleshooting, gaming, and optimizing performance.

Here's a quick recap of your PC-building journey:

1. Research and Planning: You began by researching components, setting a budget, and planning your PC build.

2. Component Selection: You carefully chose a CPU, GPU, motherboard, RAM, storage, power supply, case, and peripherals that met your requirements.

3. Assembly: You assembled your PC step by step, ensuring that all components were properly installed and connected.

4. Operating System: You installed an operating system, essential software, and drivers to make your PC functional.

5. Maintenance and Troubleshooting: You learned how to maintain your PC, troubleshoot common issues, and optimize performance.

6. PC Gaming: For gamers, you explored the exciting world of PC gaming, including graphics settings, peripherals, and game streaming.

7. Future-Proofing: Finally, you explored strategies for extending the life of your custom-built PC through future-proofing and hardware upgrades.

Your PC-building journey doesn't end here. Continue to explore new technologies, upgrade components as needed, and enjoy the flexibility and performance of your custom-built PC.

Building your own PC is not just about having a powerful machine; it's about acquiring valuable knowledge and skills that will serve you well in the world of technology. Whether you use your PC for work, creativity, gaming, or a bit of everything, your custom-built PC is a reflection of your passion and dedication to the world of computing.

Thank you for joining us on this exciting journey of building and customizing your PC. May your computer continue to serve you well and adapt to your evolving needs.

CHAPTER 11: BEYOND THE BASICS – ADVANCED PC BUILDING TECHNIQUES

As a PC enthusiast, you've already conquered the basics of building a custom PC. In this chapter, we'll delve into more advanced techniques and concepts to take your PC-building skills to the next level. These advanced practices will help you fine-tune your PC, tackle complex projects, and explore cutting-edge technologies.

11.1 Cable Management Mastery

Cable management is an art form that not only makes your PC look clean and organized but also contributes to better airflow and cooling. Here are some advanced cable management tips:

1. Modular PSU: If you're building a high-end PC, invest in a modular PSU that allows you to attach only the cables you need, reducing clutter.

2. Custom Cable Sleeving: Consider custom cable sleeving for a sleek and professional look. You can purchase pre-sleeved cables or sleeve them yourself for a truly unique appearance.

3. Cable Combs and Clips: Use cable combs and clips to keep individual cables organized and aligned, creating a neat and tidy interior.

4. Routing and Bundling: Carefully plan the routes for your cables, bundling them together where possible and using cable channels or Velcro straps to secure them.

5. Rear Cable Management: Don't neglect cable management behind the motherboard tray. Many cases have dedicated cable management areas to keep the rear side clean and clutter-free.

11.2 Advanced Cooling Solutions

While stock cooling solutions work well for most PCs, advanced cooling solutions can optimize performance and aesthetics:

1. Liquid Cooling: Consider custom liquid cooling loops for superior cooling performance and a unique visual appeal. Building a custom loop involves selecting components like water blocks, radiators, and tubing.

2. RGB Lighting: Enhance your PC's aesthetics with RGB lighting components, such as RGB fans, LED strips, and RGB-compatible motherboards. Fine-tune lighting effects to match your setup's color scheme.

3. Fan Control: Use advanced fan control software to manage fan speeds and create custom fan curves for optimized cooling and noise levels.

4. Overclocking with Precision: Advanced cooling solutions enable more aggressive overclocking, pushing your CPU and GPU to their limits while maintaining stable temperatures.

11.3 Advanced Hardware Projects

For those seeking a challenge, advanced hardware projects can take your PC-building skills to the next level:

1. Case Modding: Transform your PC case with custom modifications, including window panels, paint jobs, or even 3D-printed accessories. Case modding allows you to showcase your creativity.

2. Multi-GPU Setup: Experiment with multi-GPU setups (SLI or CrossFire) for extreme gaming performance. Be aware that multi-GPU support in modern games is limited, so research compatibility before investing.

3. Custom PCBs: For the truly adventurous, designing and building custom printed circuit boards (PCBs) for specialized applications is a complex but rewarding endeavor.

4. Extreme Cooling: Explore extreme cooling methods like liquid nitrogen (LN2) or phase change cooling to push your system to its absolute limits. Extreme cooling requires specialized equipment and safety precautions.

11.4 Staying Informed

The world of PC hardware is ever-evolving, so staying informed is essential for advanced PC builders. Here's how:

1. Online Communities: Join PC enthusiast forums, Reddit communities, and social media groups to stay updated on the latest hardware trends, discussions, and user experiences.

2. Tech News Websites: Follow tech news websites and YouTube channels dedicated to hardware reviews, benchmarks, and analysis.

3. Conventions and Events: Attend computer hardware conventions and events like CES (Consumer Electronics Show) to see cutting-edge technology in action and network with fellow enthusiasts.

4. Hands-On Learning: Continue to build and experiment with various PC configurations to gain practical experience and deepen your understanding.

5. Advanced Certifications: Consider pursuing advanced certifications like CompTIA's A+ or CompTIA's Network+ to validate your knowledge and skills in the field of IT.

Advanced PC building is a journey of continuous learning and improvement. While these techniques may seem daunting, they offer a rewarding opportunity to explore the limitless possibilities of custom PC building. Embrace the challenge, push your boundaries, and enjoy the satisfaction of mastering the art of PC construction.

Remember that advanced PC building requires patience, careful planning, and attention to detail. Whether you're aiming for a showpiece PC with breathtaking aesthetics or pursuing extreme performance, the world of advanced PC building is yours to explore and conquer.

CHAPTER 12: THE SUSTAINABLE PC BUILDER

In this chapter, we'll explore how to approach PC building with sustainability in mind. Sustainable PC building focuses on minimizing environmental impact, extending the life of your components, and making eco-conscious choices throughout the PC's lifecycle.

12.1 Sustainable Component Choices

When building a sustainable PC, consider the following component choices:

1. Energy-Efficient Components: Opt for power-efficient components, such as CPUs and GPUs with lower TDP (thermal design power). These components consume less electricity, reducing your PC's carbon footprint.

2. Modular Design: Choose components that are easy to disassemble and repair, promoting longevity. Look for modular motherboards, power supplies, and cases that allow for component upgrades and replacements.

3. Recycled Materials: Some manufacturers use recycled materials in their components and packaging. Support these eco-friendly initiatives when selecting hardware.

4. Extended Warranty: Consider components with extended warranties, as this can encourage manufacturers to create products that are built to last.

12.2 Repurposing and Upcycling

Sustainable PC building doesn't always require buying new components. Consider the following approaches:

1. Repurposing Old Hardware: Instead of discarding old PCs, repurpose them for secondary tasks like media centers, home servers, or educational machines. Older hardware can still be valuable in these roles.

2. Upcycling: Get creative with upcycling projects. Turn outdated computer parts into functional or decorative items. For example, old RAM sticks can become keychains, and hard drives can be used as wall clocks.

12.3 Energy Efficiency

Efficient energy use is a cornerstone of sustainability. Follow these tips to reduce your PC's energy consumption:

1. Power Management: Configure your operating system to use power-saving features when the PC is idle. This includes putting the monitor and hard drives to sleep when not in use.

2. Scheduled Shutdowns: If your PC is used intermittently, schedule automatic shutdowns during times when it's not needed.

3. LED Lighting: If you use RGB lighting, adjust brightness and colors to minimize energy use. Turn off lighting when it's not needed.

12.4 E-Waste Recycling

E-waste (electronic waste) is a growing environmental concern. Here's how you can responsibly manage e-waste:

1. Recycling Programs: Many regions have recycling programs or drop-off locations for electronics. Research local options for recycling old PC components and devices.

2. Donations: Consider donating functional but no longer needed hardware to schools, charities, or individuals who can use them.

3. Proper Disposal: If recycling or donation isn't possible, ensure proper disposal by taking your e-waste to a designated facility. Do not throw electronics in the regular trash.

12.5 Software Efficiency

Sustainability also involves efficient software usage:

1. Minimalist Software: Use lightweight software alternatives when possible. They consume fewer system resources and energy.

2. Virtualization: If you need multiple operating systems or environments, consider virtualization. Virtual machines can reduce the need for multiple physical PCs.

3. Cloud Storage: Use cloud storage for file backups and sharing. This can reduce the need for local storage, saving both energy and resources.

12.6 Green Computing Practices

Embrace green computing practices as part of your sustainable PC-building journey:

1. Reduce, Reuse, Recycle: Follow the "reduce, reuse, recycle" mantra when it comes to PC components and electronic devices.

2. Eco-Friendly Accessories: Choose eco-friendly peripherals like keyboards and mice made from sustainable materials.

3. Energy-Efficient Monitors: Select monitors with high energy efficiency ratings, such as ENERGY STAR-certified displays.

4. Sustainable Power: Consider powering your PC with renewable energy sources like solar or wind if feasible.

Building a sustainable PC is not only good for the environment but also aligns with the principles of responsible consumption and resource conservation. By making eco-conscious choices throughout the PC-building process and the lifecycle of your system, you can contribute to a more sustainable future for the planet. Remember that every small step counts, and your efforts can inspire others to adopt sustainable practices in their PC-building endeavors.

APPENDIX A: PC COMPONENT COMPATIBILITY GUIDE

One of the key aspects of building a PC is ensuring that all your components are compatible with each other. Here's a quick reference guide to help you understand component compatibility:

CPU and Motherboard Compatibility:
- Check the motherboard's socket type (e.g., LGA 1151, AM4) to ensure it matches your CPU.
- Ensure the motherboard supports the CPU's generation (e.g., 10th Gen Intel or Ryzen 5000 series).

GPU Compatibility:
- Verify that the GPU physically fits in your case. Measure the available space and compare it to the GPU's dimensions.
- Ensure the power supply can provide the required wattage and connectors for your GPU.

RAM Compatibility:
- Check the motherboard's memory type (e.g., DDR4 or DDR5) and maximum supported speed.
- Ensure the RAM modules are compatible with the motherboard and are of the correct type (e.g., DIMM or SO-DIMM).

Storage Compatibility:
- Ensure the motherboard has the necessary M.2 or SATA

connectors for your SSDs and HDDs.

- Confirm the form factor and interface of your storage devices (e.g., NVMe, SATA).

Power Supply Compatibility:
- Calculate your PC's power requirements based on the components you're using.
- Ensure the power supply has the necessary connectors and wattage to support your components.

Case Compatibility:
- Check the case's form factor (e.g., ATX, microATX) and ensure it matches your motherboard.
- Ensure the case has enough space for your components and any potential upgrades.

Cooling Compatibility:
- Verify that CPU coolers and GPU coolers fit within the case without obstruction.
- Ensure that the case supports the installation of additional cooling solutions, like fans or liquid cooling radiators.

Remember to consult your component manuals and the manufacturer's websites for specific compatibility details when building your PC.

APPENDIX B: TROUBLESHOOTING GUIDE

Sometimes, PC builders encounter issues that require troubleshooting. Here's a troubleshooting guide to help you identify and resolve common problems:

1. No Power:
- Check power connections, including the PSU switch and wall outlet.
- Ensure the PSU is functional. Test with another PSU if possible.

2. No Display:
- Verify that the monitor is connected and powered on.
- Check the GPU and RAM seating. Re-seat if necessary.
- Test with a different display cable or monitor.

3. Blue Screen of Death (BSOD):
- Note the error code displayed on the BSOD for reference.
- Update or reinstall faulty drivers.
- Check for hardware issues like RAM or overheating.

4. Overheating:
- Ensure proper airflow and cooling inside the case.
- Check CPU and GPU temperatures with monitoring software.
- Reapply thermal paste if temperatures are too high.

5. Software Crashes:
- Update or reinstall problematic software.
- Check for conflicts between software applications.
- Scan for malware that may be causing instability.

6. Internet Connection Issues:
- Restart your router and modem.
- Check for loose cables and try a wired connection if possible.
- Contact your ISP for assistance with connection problems.

7. Noisy Fans:
- Clean or replace dusty or malfunctioning fans.
- Adjust fan curves in the BIOS/UEFI settings to reduce noise.

For more in-depth troubleshooting, consult the manufacturer's support resources, PC forums, or seek assistance from experienced PC builders.

APPENDIX C: RESOURCES AND FURTHER READING

Building and maintaining a PC involves continuous learning. Here are some resources and reading materials to help you expand your knowledge:

Online Communities:
- Reddit's r/buildapc: A community for PC builders to seek advice and share experiences.
- Tom's Hardware Forums: A platform for discussions, troubleshooting, and hardware reviews.

Tech News Websites:
- AnandTech: In-depth hardware reviews and analysis.
- Ars Technica: News and in-depth reports on technology and PC components.

PC Building Guides:
- PCPartPicker (pcpartpicker.com): A valuable tool for selecting compatible components and browsing user builds.
- Linus Tech Tips (YouTube channel): Informative videos on PC building, hardware reviews, and tech news.

Books:
- "The Art of Electronics" by Paul Horowitz and Winfield Hill: A comprehensive guide to electronics and circuits.
- "Upgrading and Repairing PCs" by Scott

Mueller: A comprehensive reference for PC hardware and troubleshooting.

Certifications:

- CompTIA A+ Certification: A widely recognized certification for IT professionals, covering PC hardware, software, and troubleshooting.
- CompTIA Network+ Certification: Focuses on networking concepts, including configuring and managing network devices.

These resources can help you stay informed about the latest technology trends, troubleshoot issues, and expand your PC-building skills.

These appendices provide valuable reference material to complement the knowledge you've gained throughout the book. They cover component compatibility, troubleshooting common issues, and point you toward additional resources for further learning and exploration in the world of PC building.

CONCLUSION: EMBARK ON YOUR PC BUILDING JOURNEY

In this comprehensive guide to building a PC, we've explored the exciting world of custom PC creation from start to finish. We've covered everything from selecting components and assembly to software installation, maintenance, gaming, performance optimization, advanced techniques, sustainability, and ethical considerations.

Now, let's recap some key takeaways from your PC building journey:

1. Customization: Building your own PC allows you to create a personalized computing powerhouse tailored to your needs and preferences. Whether you're a gamer, a creative professional, or someone who needs a reliable workhorse, your custom-built PC can meet your unique requirements.

2. Knowledge and Skills: Throughout this journey, you've gained valuable knowledge and skills in hardware selection, assembly, software installation, maintenance, and troubleshooting. These skills empower you to take control of your technology and solve problems effectively.

3. Performance Optimization: You've learned how to optimize your PC for peak performance, whether for gaming, productivity, or other tasks. From overclocking to advanced cooling solutions, you have the tools to fine-tune your PC.

4.Sustainability: We've discussed the importance of sustainability and ethical considerations in PC building. By making eco-conscious and socially responsible choices, you can contribute to a better world while enjoying the benefits of your custom PC.

5.Ethical PC Building: Consider the ethical implications of your choices, from component selection to software usage and disposal of e-waste. Ethical PC building is about aligning your actions with values that promote fairness, inclusivity, and responsible consumption.

6. Continuous Learning: The world of PC hardware and technology is ever-evolving. Stay curious and keep learning, whether through online communities, tech news websites, books, or certifications.

Now, it's time to encourage you to embark on your own PC building journey, if you haven't already. Building a PC isn't just about assembling components; it's about taking control of your technology and embracing a world of endless possibilities. It's about personalization, empowerment, and self-discovery.

No matter your experience level, whether you're a novice or an experienced builder, there's always room to grow and explore. Building a PC is not just a one-time project; it's an ongoing journey of learning and self-improvement in the ever-evolving world of technology.

So, gather your enthusiasm, do your research, plan your build, and take that first step. Assemble your components, install your operating system, and make your PC your own. Enjoy the satisfaction of seeing your creation come to life and the pride of saying, "I built this."

Embrace the challenges, celebrate the victories, and remember that every hurdle you overcome brings you closer to becoming a true PC-building enthusiast. Whether you're building a PC for work, play, creativity, or a combination of all three, your journey is just beginning, and the possibilities are limitless.

Thank you for joining us on this remarkable adventure of PC building. May your custom-built PC serve you well, and may your passion for technology continue to grow. Happy building!

ABOUT THE AUTHOR

Ross Pelayo has been an avid enthusiast and passionate PC builder for the past two decades. With a deep-seated love for technology and a keen eye for detail, they have dedicated their time to mastering the art of PC assembly, customization, and optimization.

Over the years, Ross has witnessed the evolution of computer hardware and software, from the early days of towering desktops to the sleek and powerful machines of today. Their extensive experience has not only fueled their own PC-building journey but has also inspired them to share their knowledge with others
.

As a firm believer in the transformative power of technology, Ross has helped countless individuals embark on their own PC-building adventures, whether for gaming, work, or creative pursuits. They continue to stay at the forefront of technological advancements, always eager to explore new possibilities and push the boundaries of what a custom-built PC can achieve.

Through their unwavering dedication to the world of PC building, Ross has cultivated a rich understanding of the intricate balance between innovation, sustainability, and ethics in the realm of technology. Their passion for building and their commitment to responsible practices shine brightly in the pages of this book.

Join Ross on this journey through the fascinating world of PC building and discover the joy, empowerment, and endless potential that building your own PC can bring. With two decades of experience under their belt, they are your trusted guide to a fulfilling and rewarding PC-building adventure.

www.ingramcontent.com/pod-product-compliance
Lightning Source LLC
LaVergne TN
LVHW010040070326
832903LV00071B/4438